Modern Tactical Development

by
Allen Wade

D1008082

Published by
REEDSWAIN, INC.

Library of Congress Cataloging - in - Publication Data

Wade, Allen
  Modern Tactical Development/Allen Wade

ISBN No. 09651020-5-X
Copyright © 1996 Allen Wade

Reprinted from the book <u>The F.A. Guide to Training and Coaching</u> with permission from The Football Association.

Reedswain books are available at special discounts for bulk purchase. For details, contact the Special Sales Manager at Reedswain.

Printed in the United States of America.

REEDSWAIN INC
612 Pughtown Road · Spring City PA 19475
1-800-331-5191

Table of Contents

Introduction

There are, reputedly, two stages through which worthwhile ideas must pass before they are accepted. In the first stage they are ignored, in the second, ridiculed. Coaching has passed through these stages and is now accepted as a necessary process in the education and development of more skillful players at all levels. Indeed, if this were not so, the whole process of education from early school years to university level could be viewed with doubts and reservations.

A coach's aim is to find the most economical way of causing a player to become a better player in the widest possible sense. This improvement may relate to the player's understanding of the game or to the development of his technique. More likely it concerns a combination of both: indeed these two aspects of a player's capabilities must be interdependent.

In the past, coaching was ignored because the reservoirs of so-called natural talent seemed limitless. It was subsequently ridiculed, probably because some players, eminent in their time, had not been taught, so it was assumed that no-one could be taught. Had this belief prevailed in the musical field, the development of great instrumentalists would surely have been under a handicap.

This book has been written to present the experience of The Football Association over the years in the fields of coaching and training. The knowledge gained has been, and will continue to be, tested and tried, as new ideas emerge and changes occur. The main purpose of the book is not to provide categorical answers or suggest cut-and-dried methods; answers and methods are not so easily arrived at. Its purpose is to present ideas and principles which will require coaches to think. They, in turn, must provoke thought and enquiry among their players. Unthinking coaches and players mean, ultimately, stagnation in the game. Stagnation produces complacency and this must never again be permitted to occur in this country.

A.W.

Acknowledgment

The Football Association depends upon the unselfish and often unsparing efforts of a great many people for the success of its instructional work. The coaching scheme is the result of the intelligence, skill, and soccer 'know how' of men from all the different levels at which the game is played. To a great extent this book is an attempt to sum up their experience and, as a consequence, my sincere thanks are given to everyone who has contributed to the development of coaching in England. In particular, my thanks are due to the Staff Coaches of The Football Association. These are the men who are responsible for the National Coaching Courses; men who have provided and who continue to provide so much inspiration in the cause of skillful soccer.

The preparation of this book would have been considerably hindered without the cheerful effort lavished upon it by my secretary, Joan Pritchard. To her and to the many others who have assisted me, may I express my gratitude.

Modern Tactical Development

Tactics are modifications or adaptations of play within a team system and they will be affected by the following considerations.

1. Skills of the individual players in the team.
2. Deficiency of skills in the individual team players.
3. Skills of the opposing players.
4. Lack of skills in the opposing players.
5. Ground and weather conditions.
6. Injuries to one's own players and to opposing players.
7. The degree of understanding within a team (for example, use of rehearsed movements during play and particularly at throw-in, free-kick, corner-kick, etc.).
8. The state of the game.

Let us look at some examples of the way in which tactics can be affected by the above considerations. Let us imagine that our wingers are both clever ball-players who are capable of beating opponents with the ball but who are not fast runners either with the ball or without it. Tactically, therefore, we should modify our system of play to make the most of these players' skill with the ball and to disguise their lack of speed. Long passes over the opposing full-backs will be a waste of time except where the wingers have tempted the full-backs into positions remote from their goal. These long passes will be made into the space behind the backs for the center-forward or perhaps one of the inside-forwards, to run onto. During attacking phases of the game we may decide that the wingers can be used to the greatest advantage nearest to the opponents' penalty-area. If we are able to pass the ball to them in wide positions in this part of the field we may be able to create a situation where they can use their dribbling ability to beat the opposing full-backs and so to turn the flanks of the defense. In this part of the field we may ask our other attackers to deliberately move away from the wingers in order to draw away covering defenders. Similarly, we may find that one of our wingers has a marked ability to beat a full-back by going outside him or down the line. Where this is so, we need to ensure that the path down the line is clear of other players.

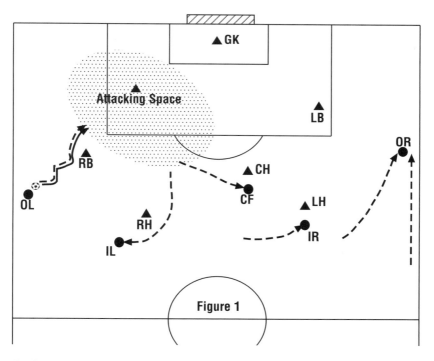

Figure 1

In *fig.* 1 the forwards have moved away from the OL in such a way as to try to clear the space behind the RB and also to draw defenders away from covering positions. In this way they are helping the OL to establish a position in which he can beat the opposing RB.

In *fig.* 2 where the OL may be capable of beating his full-back on the inside, the other forwards have moved to assist him. The IL has moved behind the RB to the wing (thus maintaining width in attack), trying to draw the RH away from a central covering position. Similarly the other forwards have tried to draw defenders away from the center part of the field in front of the penalty-area into which the OL must go if he succeeds in beating his full-back. In this way our tactics are being adapted to suit the players' skill, their ability to dribble round opponents, and to disguise their weakness

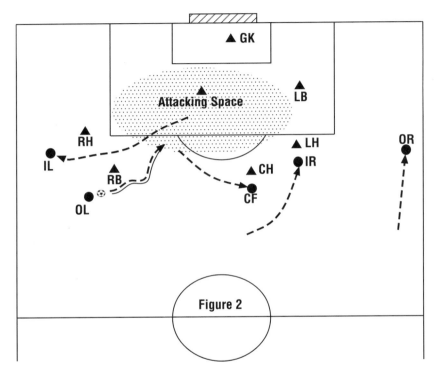

Figure 2

(inability to run fast with and without the ball). A further example of a players weakness requiring disguise through an adaptation of tactics would arise if our center-half were not too confident at heading when challenged. This is obviously a serious weakness for a central defensive player. We might require one of the wing half-backs to drop into a covering role behind the center-half whenever high passes are made in his direction down the center of the field. Where high crosses are coming from the wings we might arrange for the center-forward to be marked by one of the wing half-backs with the center-half adopting a covering position as in *fig*. 3. All that we are doing is trying to make sure that the player is rarely, if ever, in a position where his weakness can be exposed.

During a match we should read certain aspects of the opposing team's play. The general pattern of their play should be recognized and, after a while, the styles of individual players noted. Tactically, we must exploit their weaknesses. For example, one of the opposing wing half-backs may be inclined to get drawn out to the wing. When the wing-man receives the ball the RH, for example, tends to challenge him if he is near enough. An attempt to exploit this weakness tactically might involve our IL moving out to extreme wing positions both behind and in front of the OL.

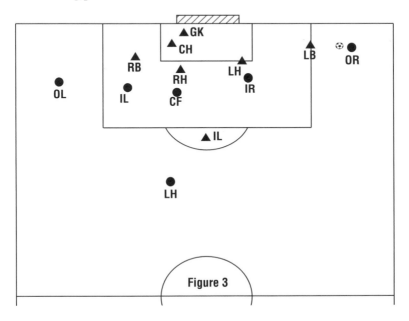

Figure 3

In *fig.* 4 the IL has moved behind the OL and the RH can challenge the OL, as he is inclined to do, since he can see both the IL and the OL. In doing so he is leaving a large space in the center of the field. The RB dare not come forward to fill this gap since he will leave the RH uncovered. If, by good understanding, either of the two wing half-backs can read this situation, they can make a quick break into this dangerous space. By being drawn away from a central defensive position the RH is ignoring the principles of defensive play. Other forwards have assisted by 'moving off the ball', to draw defenders from covering positions.

Frequently, it is difficult to spot weaknesses in an opposing side and in these circumstances it may be necessary to direct our attention to their strongest aspects of play. A team is confident in doing the things it can do well. To play on the strength of a team is to try to encourage it to become over-confident.

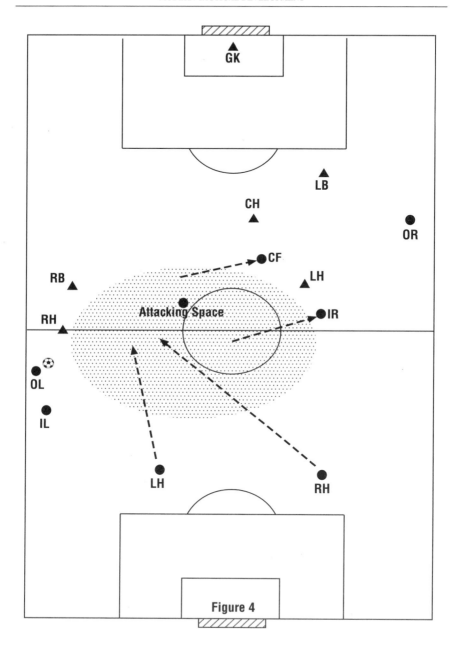

Figure 4

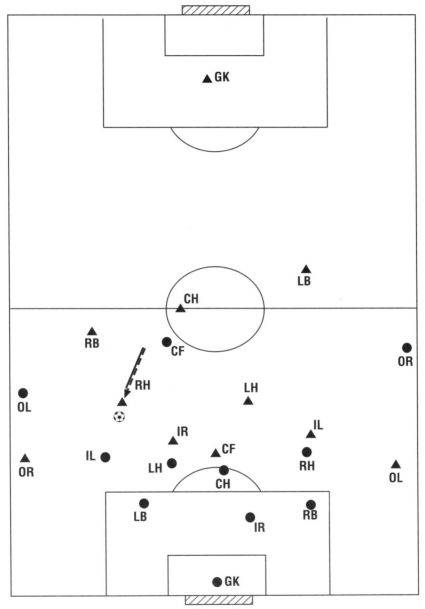

Figure 5

Let us imagine ourselves up against players who are showing themselves to be a strong attacking side. Individually and collectively they are quick and accurate and possess eleven dribblers; also they can shoot. We might decide to encourage them to attack by falling back or retreating to the edge of our penalty-area where we set up a defensive structure of seven or eight players. Our aim is to draw more and more of the opposing players into attacking movements. Our defensive aim is to restrict the amount of free space within our defense and to restrict the movement of attacking players behind us. When a side is heavily committed to attack, it is most vulnerable to counter-attack since there is the maximum amount of space behind the rearmost defenders (*fig.* 5).

To encourage heavy attacking play we might ask both our inside forwards to adopt deep defensive positions (for example, *fig.* 5) in order to

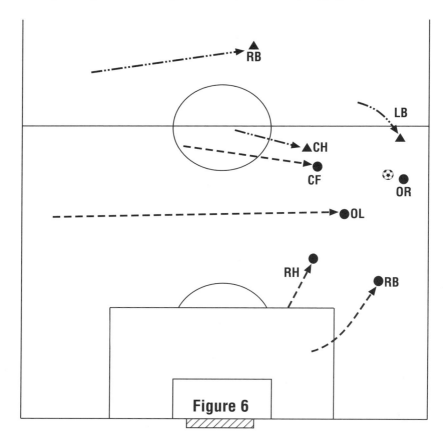

Figure 6

encourage the opposing wing half-backs into advanced attacking movements. If the ball can now be played from defense quickly we have established possession of the ball in a three against three situation where our OR, CF, and OL are opposed by the LB, CH, and RB. If our three forwards can support each other quickly a rapid break-through may be achieved. Since both inside forwards have taken up deep defensive positions when the break is made it must be quickly supported by the nearest defensive players.

In *fig.* 6 the OL and the CF have moved across to the OR to whom a clearance has been made. In order to exploit the quick break through it may be necessary for both the RB and the RH to support this attacking move.

Ground and weather conditions will obviously affect match tactics considerably. Players with only average ball control are made to look much better than they are on soft grounds. On hard, bumpy grounds and particularly in strong winds the same players are in difficulty. The type of pass to be used will also be affected by different playing conditions. On a firm ground, with a wet top, players can increase the range of their ground passes by as much as twenty-five yards. On a very soft ground the range of effective ground passes is reduced considerably with the added danger of the ball sticking half way to its target. It should be no surprise to find many teams playing better soccer against a strong wind, than with the wind behind them. Against the wind the ball has to be kept low and therefore players are often forced to support each other rather more closely. When playing with the wind there is a temptation to let the passes go more freely with the result that forward players tend to remain in more advanced positions. This causes the team to become stretched and often a gap appears between the 'feeders' and the 'chasers'.

Here are other sets of conditions which can affect basic team play. On a wet but firm ground where the greasy top surface allows the ball to skid through easily, defenders are in trouble when they are made to turn. This means that the ball can be pushed through to attacking players with a great degree of accuracy and a greater range of passing distance. At the same time the use of quick, square passing in attack can cause difficulties for the attacking side since the slightest inaccuracy will cause the receiver to have to turn under extreme difficulties. Build-up play should be to the receiver's feet and, preferably forwards or backwards rather than square. In this way the receiver is moving on to the ball and is able to assess the passing possibilities in front of him with the minimum of difficulty. Defensively, these ground conditions will mean that defenders will not be able to commit themselves so readily to interceptions or to tight marking positions.

9

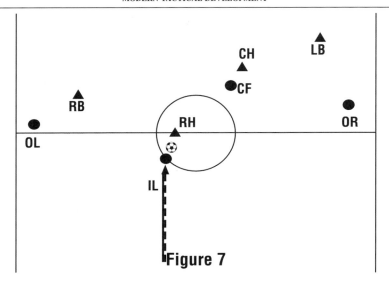

Figure 7

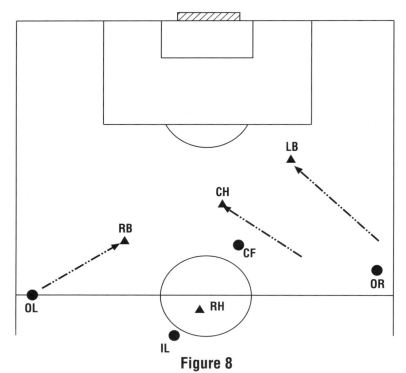

Figure 8

They will tend to take up positions well inside their opponents' in order to avoid the increased possibility of passes going through the defense on the inside of players.

In *fig.* 7 where ground conditions are firm, the RB is near to the opposing OL in order to try to intercept a pass from the IL or to make a quick tackle. The LB has assumed an orthodox covering position. The defenders can take up these positions because they know that ground conditions will allow them to turn quickly should the necessity arise.

In *fig.* 8, where playing conditions are treacherous, the RB has deliberately stood off the OL to narrow the gap between the RH and himself. Similarly, the CH has moved over into a tighter covering position and the LB has swung over to offer maximum cover to the CH. They have done this to prevent the possibility of passes being made behind and between them.

When playing against the wind, teams must support each other more closely in defense in order to cover against the possibility of the wind causing the ball to play tricks. In attacking play, therefore, considerable use may be made of the low, powerfully driven pass through the opposing defense. A ball so delivered is held by the wind thus giving advanced attackers a better chance of catching the pass.

When playing with the wind the passing range of all the players is increased through wind assistance. Cross-field passes are much more effective but down-field passes have to be measured carefully because they may run away from attackers too quickly. The chip pass is effective under these conditions since it is delivered with a minimum amount of forward movement and the height achieved allows the wind to carry the ball thus causing difficulty to defenders.

When playing with a strong wind players tend to forget the principle of supporting the player with the ball. This is a major fault whatever the conditions. Possibly one of the most embarrassing and difficult situations in which to play is that produced by a bright sun just before it sets, in these circumstances attacking teams will deliberately build up play so that passes into dangerous parts of the field are delivered with the sun shining from behind the passes. This means that it shines into the eyes of defending players. On any away ground it is worth finding out:

    1. Which way the prevailing wind blows
    2. From which direction the sun shines at various times during
       the afternoon.

Both minor and major injuries are to be expected in a game and they are part and parcel of the game. As such they must seriously affect not only tactics but the basic system of play. So far as injuries to one's own team are concerned there are certain basic rules which apply:

1. If a player cannot move about with a fair degree of freedom he should not remain on the field. The long term consequences of a further aggravation of an injury do not warrant risks being taken.
2. Where the injury is of a minor nature the player should be used in a position in which he will cause the maximum trouble to the opposing team.

Some people advocate moving an injured player to the wing where he will be least involved in play. If this is the argument then by the same token he will cause the least trouble to the opposing side and, at the same time, he will unbalance attacking play. If he is moved to the center-forward position he cannot be ignored by the opposition, and, at the same time, passes can be made to him which enable him to pass the ball to other players with the least possible inconvenience. The attack also has the best possible balance under these circumstances. Different minor injuries affect a player's playing performance in different ways. Leg injuries make running, quick starting, and kicking difficult. Injuries to the hips and lower back make twisting and turning difficult. Obviously, recognition of these factors will cause the opposing team to try to make the injured player do whatever is most difficult by playing on his weakness. It may be thought that the tactical exploitation of an injured player is morally wrong. Extended to a logical conclusion this would mean that any game in which a player has been injured should be replayed when the sides are of equal strength. Any player who stays on the field when he has been injured does so with the aim of playing a part in team play to the best of his capabilities. One side must aim to use his limitations to advantage, the other side must expose these limitations. These factors not apparently directly concerned with the game of soccer have to be recognized in tactical adaptation.

One of the most important aspects of tactical development involves establishing a numerical advantage. Whether in attack or defense, a team must aim at having at least one extra man. In attack this will mean that however tight the marking by opposing defenders, one man is free to support or press home the advantage. It may be that the numerical superiority refers to a brief moment in time and a small space in which two attackers are able to interpass and beat one defender. The same superiority may be established during a full attacking movement which is supported from a deep defensive position. A full-back may suddenly join in an advanced attacking movement for example. In defense the extra man may be involved in deflecting the opposing attack across the field to less dangerous areas or he may be responsible for covering gaps rather than for marking specific opposing players.

Whatever the phase of the game a numerical advantage must be the aim and, once it has been established, its exploitation depends upon one thing alone: accuracy in passing. It has often been said that if a player cannot pass accurately and with control he cannot really play soccer. Certainly, all the possibilities for combined tactical play depend to a great extent upon this technique. The ability to direct a pass exactly where it is intended to go, at the right speed, with just enough spin or swerve if they are required, is of major importance to all players from the goalkeeper to the outside left.

Where we are concerned with the exploitation of numerical superiority irrespective of the actual number of players involved, what we are really concerned with is the establishment and exploitation of a two-against-one situation.

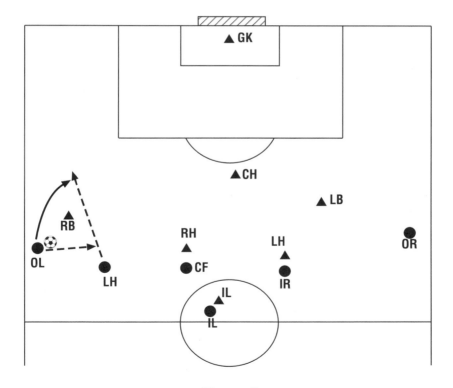

Figure 9

In *fig.* 9 where six players are defending against six attackers the movement of the LH in close support of his OL has, in that phase of wing play, created a two-against-one situation. In other words although the total numbers are equal, momentarily, a numerical advantage has been established. This situation can be created if nearby players are willing to support the player who is in possession of the ball.

SUPPORTING OR ZONING ON THE BALL

Whenever a player receives the ball he should have already assessed the situation around him and he should have made a selection from the passing opportunities available. A good player will read the game wherever the ball may be, and however unlikely it seems that he will be involved in play immediately. In this way he tries to be one, two, or three moves ahead all the time. He may receive the ball when rapid changes of play are happening and there is much movement of players around him. In these 'tight' situations he may not have time to make accurate and controlled judgements. Obviously, therefore, if he has only one player to whom he can pass he has no choice. If he has three or four, the position is simplified for him. These choices can only be possible if players move towards the player towards whom the ball is being played rather than away from him. One often hears the expression 'they had the luck or the run of the ball'. It is only possible for a team to have the run of the ball if that team has sufficient players there to whom the ball can run. This movement of supporting players towards the man with the ball achieves two things. It simplifies his choice of passing possibilities and also draws opponents in the same direction. This in itself assists the player with the ball. If, for example, he had decided on a long forward pass, zoning on the ball causes opponents to be drawn away from marking and covering positions. Thus his long pass may have an enhanced chance of success.

SETTING-UP PLAY

A team which plays controlled, methodical soccer will often employ deliberate passing movements which appear to have little or no purpose so far as scoring goals is concerned. They may deliberately interpass to draw opponents towards the ball. They do this in order to create openings for a through-pass towards their opponents' goal.

In *fig.* 10 the IR has passed to the CF moving towards him and who is being tightly marked by the CH. The CF then gives a return pass at an angle and turns away from the center of the field. The pass has been set up with the intention of drawing the CH away from his goal in order that a

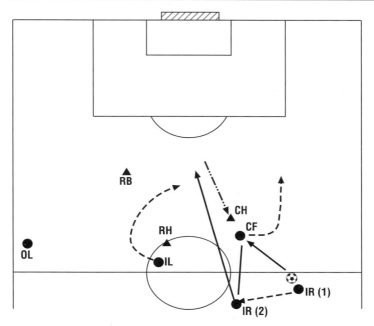

Figure 10

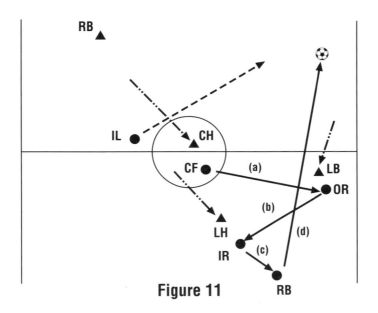

Figure 11

through-pass can be given into the space behind him.

In *fig*. 11 the IR, the CF, and the OR have all interpassed while moving towards their right-back. These setting-up passes have been aimed at drawing the opposing LH, CH, and LB down-field to create space into which the RB may play the ball, perhaps for the IL who moves off on a diagonal run behind these opposing defenders. The higher the class of soccer the more a team must use setting-up play to tempt the opposing team into making mistakes. One of the aspects of soccer which is of vital importance and yet, because it is based upon human weaknesses, is most difficult to calculate, is that involving ball possession. If a team is submitted to long periods of play in which it is denied possession of the ball, its players become anxious and take risks in trying to regain possession. At this time such a team is most vulnerable to quick counter-attack.

KEEP BALL

A recent development in top-class play has been the use of interpassing play of an apparently purposeless nature. Here a team with a commanding lead will interpass the ball in any direction and often backwards in order to slow the game down and make their opponents advance to try to regain possession. The losing team is obliged to take risks to regain possession. Its players must commit themselves to chasing the ball and opposing players. This means that players can be drawn into bad positions and that space is created between and behind defensive positions. Obviously, in these circumstances a quick counter-attack has an enhanced chance of success. Denying one's opponents possession of the ball is an important skill and demands team work of a very high order.

SQUARE PASSING

When used properly this can be an excellent means of drawing defenders. If it develops generally, however, it involves considerable risks and can lead to negative play.

In *fig*. 12 the LH and RH have interpassed square across the field with the object of drawing the opposing IR and IL into a square position. This is a position in which they are not covering each other. At the same time, they are easily exposed for a through pass. Square passing becomes negative when players use it as a first choice, in other words when they are always looking for the easy pass. This may be for two reasons. Firstly, they have got into the bad habit of not wishing to accept the responsibility for making a through pass which might be intercepted. Secondly, they may have been

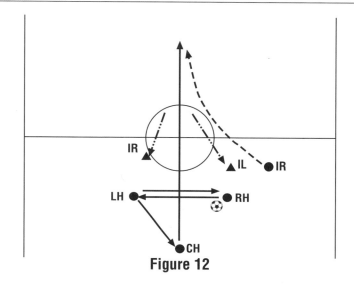

Figure 12

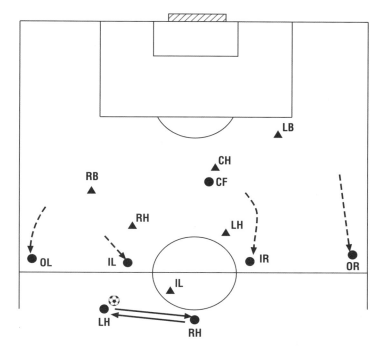

Figure 13

forced into this sort of play because other players will not take up forward positions where they may be strongly challenged .

In *fig*. 13 all the forwards with the exception of the CF want to move away from the defenders thus the LH and RH have very few opportunities to make penetration passes. This will cause interpassing movements to become negative.

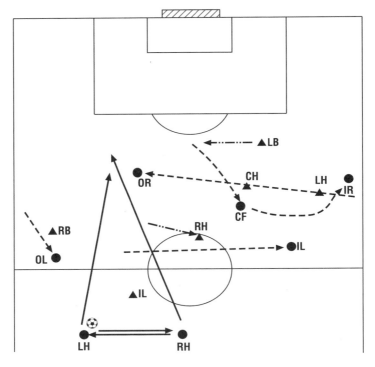

Figure 14

In fig. 14 where the OR has made a positive forward movement which has been assisted by the diagonal movements of the CF and IR there are opportunities for progressive, purposeful play. What is known as 'front running' demands a great deal of effort and considerable courage. Forward runs take players into dangerous positions and, naturally, positions in which they are likely to be tightly marked and submitted to strong physical challenge. Without front runners a team has little or no chance of effecting penetration. One will see a great deal of pretty interpassing all to no purpose.

DIAGONAL RUNNING

Reference has already been made to the need for interchange of positions in attack. Mobility in attack is a fundamental principle of the game. Any good defense will rarely, if ever, allow attacking players to run unopposed towards goal. The more that these long, through-passes are attempted, the more a defense will fall back, cover and so cut off the possibility. The higher the class of soccer, the more this is true. If players insist in always running towards goal they are making themselves difficult targets for a pass and they are also taking defenders in a direction which the defenders are most happy to take (*fig.* 15). In the diagram one can see the difficulty which faces the IR in passing to any of the other forwards particularly where the opposing team is using a sweeper center-half. The forwards who are running towards goal are helping the defense to reduce the space into which the IR wants to pass the ball. More over since they are running away from him the forwards are making an accurate pass extremely difficult.

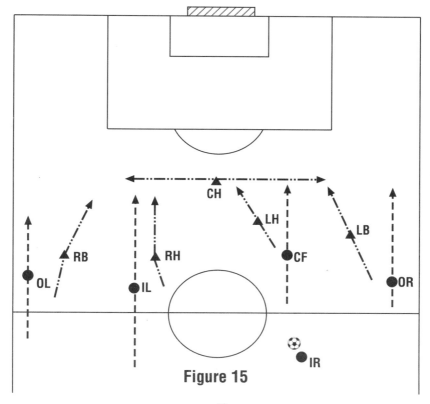

Figure 15

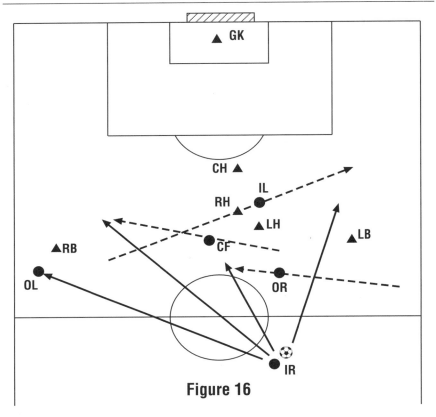

Figure 16

The diagonal movements of the forwards pose a different problem. To what extent dare the defenders now fall back and leave men unmarked? The purpose of diagonal running is to cause defenders to react by moving across the field. Better passing angles are made for the player with the ball and gaps are created through which he can pass. At the same time defenders are discouraged from retreating to reduce the space behind them. Many of these runs must be made, some of which are carried out with the intention of receiving a pass, others are undertaken to create better passing possibilities for other players. In *fig.* 16 the movement of the IL from an orthodox IL position through positions behind the opposing left-half and left-back is an example of moving in such a way. The player's main aim is to attract the attention of opposing players and if possible to draw them some of the way with him. If, for example, the RH follows him part of the way a gap has thus been opened for the CF's diagonal run into a much more dangerous position.

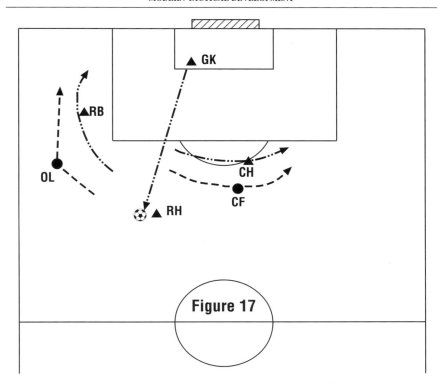

Figure 17

MOVEMENT OFF THE BALL

The kind of running movements which have just been referred to are known as 'movements off the ball'. Moving off the ball is required of all players in as much as they must always be aware of the need to help the player in possession by making decoy movements. A simple example might be that shown in *fig.* 17. At this goal-kick both the CH and the RB can see that their RH is in a good position for a pass. The opposing OL and CF, however, are too near to the line of the pass to make it worth the risk. Seeing this the defenders both move away, calling for a pass at the same time. If they attract the opposing OL and CF with them they clear the path for a goal-kick to the RH. If the opposing players are not drawn then they themselves the RB and the CH are available for the goal-kick to be passed to them.

21

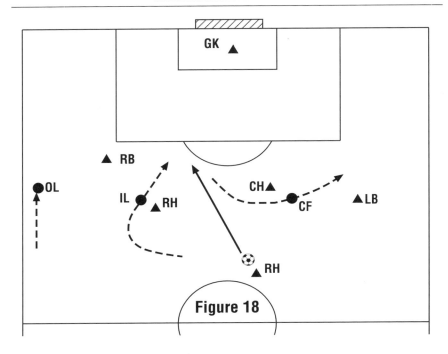

Figure 18

Another example might be that shown in *fig.* 18. Here the CF has turned away from a central position trying to draw the CH with him. By so doing he is trying to open up the line of a pass from the RH to the IL. The OL would also help by moving fairly steadily towards the corner flag trying to attract the attention of the RB. His aim would be to keep the full-back's attention away from his covering duty in the center of the field. The movements of the CF and the OL are good examples of movement off the ball since, in both cases, should the RH not feel able to make a pass to the IL, these two players are still in a position to receive a pass themselves. The aim of this sort of play is to put a defender or defenders in two minds and, ideally, to try to ensure that whichever choice the defender makes he is wrong.

In *fig.* 18 the center-half can either stay to block the run of the IL or he can cover the CF. If he fails to do the former an immediate path to goal is open. If he lets the CF go then the CF may receive an effective pass. This is an excellent example of the extent to which the calculation of risk is an important skill. A decision has to be made in a split second if the runs of the attacking players are well timed.

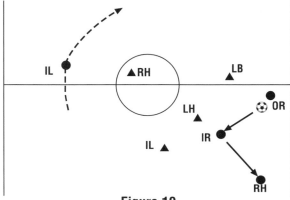

Figure 19

BLIND SIDE PLAY

We have already seen how some players tend to become 'ball watchers'. They are easily distracted from their defensive duties within the defensive organization by the player with the ball. One result of this is that it allows opposing attackers to move on to the defender's blind side (*fig*. 19).

In this diagram the RH has lost sight of the opposing IL by having his attention drawn to the interplay between the opposing RH, IR and OR. This has allowed the IL to move past him on the side nearest to the goal. At all times when defending players should try to position themselves in such a way as to see nearby attackers and the ball at the same time.

In *fig*. 20 the LH has been drawn towards the OR and he has allowed the opposing IR to move on to his blind side. The RH however has positioned

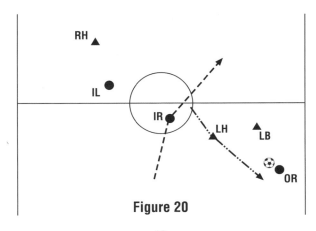

Figure 20

himself so that he can watch the ball, the opposing IL, and general play all at the same time. One of the main aims in attacking play is for forwards to get into blind side positions and particularly behind defenders.

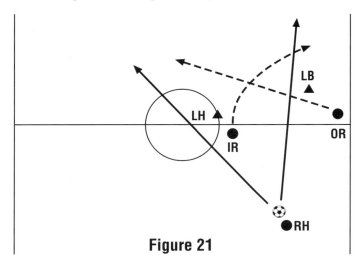

Figure 21

CROSS-OVER PLAYS

These are diagonal runs made to achieve blind side positions and which are often worked out between two or more players.

In *fig.* 21 the RH has the ball. The IR runs behind the LB and as he does so the OR moves across and behind him into the IR position. Momentarily, the defenders may be taken by surprise and one or both of the attackers may find himself free for a pass from the RH.

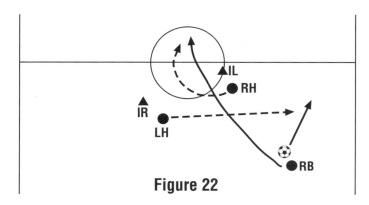

Figure 22

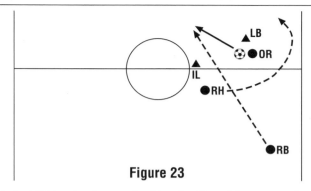

Figure 23

In *fig.* 22 the RH is closely watched by the IL and is not a safe passing possibility for the RB. The LH runs diagonally in front of the IL hoping to take the IR with him. Meanwhile, the RH turns and runs diagonally in the opposite direction, perhaps freeing himself for a pass from the RB.

A final example (*fig.* 23) shows the OR being challenged by the opposing LB. The RH is tightly marked but runs to the wing behind the OR taking the IL with him. The RB seeing that the way is now clear runs across the RH for a pass in the inside right position. As with all passing movements the timing of the players' running movements is of major importance to cause the maximum disorganization in the opposing defense.

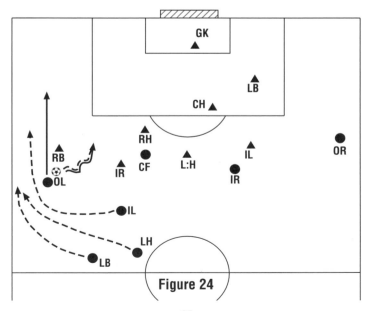

Figure 24

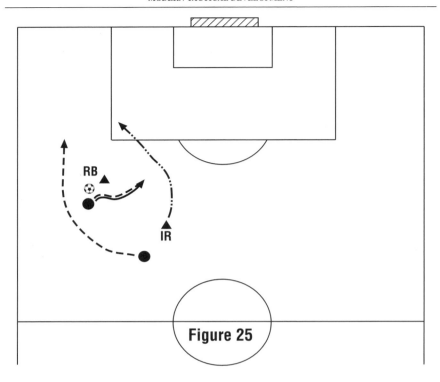

Figure 25

OVERLAPPING RUNS AND RUNS FROM
BEHIND ATTACKING PLAYERS

The need for surprise and also for creating situations in which, numerically, an attacking side has an advantage, are important aspects of attacking play. Where a defense is well organized, the defenders will be adept at moving so far to mark attackers and then leaving them to other defenders. They will also be acutely conscious of any attempt to move behind them. Overlapping runs are often used to try to turn the defense, in these circumstances.

In *fig.* 24 the defense is numerically very strong and able to mark opponents tightly and cover well. To produce an overlap the OL who is in possession of the ball moves in-field towards the opposing right-back. The CF and IR move slightly away from the left-wing principally to reduce the cover on that flank. The overlap can then be made by either the IL, the LB, or LH running outside the OL and down the line. The OL can now play the ball down the wing or, if the RB is clever enough to block this possibility, he can try to beat the RB on the inside.

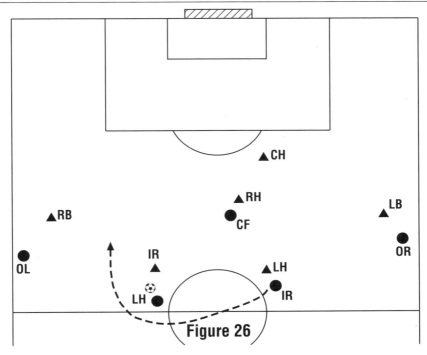

Figure 26

If the IR drops back to cover the pass down the wing the way is open for the OL to move inside (*fig.* 25). If the IR attempts to cover this possibility then he must leave the pass down the touch line as a good possibility. The use of overlapping runs is an excellent way of achieving extra men in tight playing situations and, at the same time, a high degree of mobility in attacking play. The success of this move lies in the fact that opponents do not pay so much attention to a supporting player's movement when it is behind the player with the ball.

In *fig.* 26 the passing possibilities for the LH are very limited, the opposing defense is marking tightly and covering well. Should the IR move away from the opposing LH and behind his own LH, it is unlikely that he will be followed and he may thus produce an overlap position against the IR and, at the same time, possibly expose the opposing RB to a two-against-one situation.

The use of defenders making surprise attacking runs will play an increasing part against heavy defensive systems of play. From deep positions they are able to gather speed over a long distance and they are able to create surprise by choosing their moment when to support the attack.

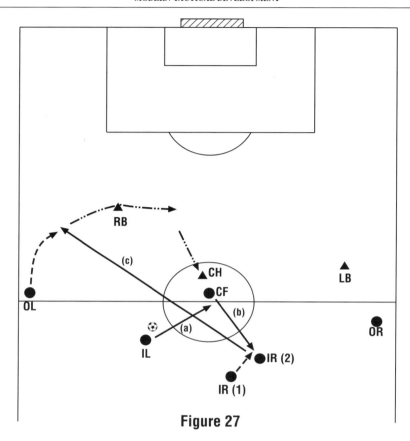

Figure 27

REVERSE PASSING

Defense is concerned with reducing the amount of space through which and into which passes can be made, and also with restricting the scope to move of attacking players. Defense is concerned with setting problems and the responsibility for doing something about this is fairly and squarely on the shoulders of the attacking side. In order to try to create attacking space and at the same time to lull defenders into a false sense of security, the direction of the attack must be changed frequently and rapidly. The reverse pass involves movement of the ball in one direction and a sudden reversal of the direction in which the ball and play generally has been moving.

In *fig.* 27 play has developed from left to right. The IL has passed to the CF who has pushed a pass back to the IR. All these players are moving in

28

the same direction. The defense will tend to move across in the same direction to cover attacking developments on that side of the field. The IR then hits a long reverse pass to the outside-left since defensive pressure has been removed from that flank.

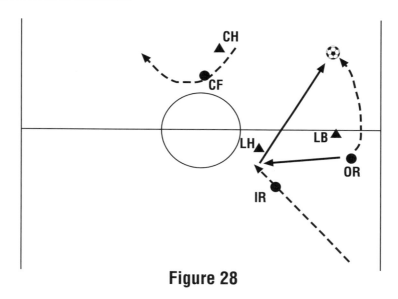

Figure 28

A common situation in which a reverse pass can be used with telling effect is between the wing-man and his inside-forward (*fig.* 28).

Having received a pass from the OR the IR makes ground towards the center of the field away from his OR. He then makes a reverse pass behind the opposing LB which his OR can run on to. Notice how the CF has assisted by drawing the CH away from a position in which he can cover the LB. This is another example of intelligent movement off the ball.

CHANGING THE PACE OF A GAME

One of the major difficulties involved in playing the traditionally open or long-passing and fast-running game is that it tends to become a one pace game. Since fast, longish passes have to be delivered quickly, inaccuracy is likely to occur. This in turn means that attacking players tend to begin their attacking runs early in order to get a start on opponents. The more inaccurate the pass the earlier they tend to run with the result that the pace of the game becomes faster and hence more inaccurate. This type of soccer may be exciting to watch but it is a bad risk and when accuracy deteriorates the game becomes a shambles. Long passes are extremely important to good soccer provided that they are used when the possibility for being accurate and therefore successful is at its greatest.

A team which plays this type of game consistently, quickly attunes the opposing team to its speed. Very little surprise is possible since the pace of the game has little variation. Attacking players are in some difficulty since they have no time themselves in which to read the developments in play which take place behind them. They know that the ball will be delivered quickly and powerfully and that they must be prepared to run early.

Slowing the pace of the game does not necessarily mean that players take more time over movements; this would result in casual play which can lead to people being caught in possession of the ball and to passes being intercepted. Slowing the pace or the game is mainly achieved by changing the direction of play away from the opposing team. Safe passes are made with no immediately apparent intention of penetrating the opposing defense. This achieves the following purposes. There are a number of players near to the ball and therefore any one of these is likely to have time in which to make the penetration pass in a controlled way. Opponents are likely to be deceived into standing still or even into being drawn away from the goal which they are defending. Since there appears to be no immediate threat from the apparently purposeless interpassing their defensive concentration may lapse. Changing the pace of a game is usually achieved by mid-field players and those behind them. This is a relatively safe part of the field since mistakes can be covered particularly when a group of four or five players is involved in interpassing.

In *fig*. 29 the team in possession is slowing the game down through static interpassing between OL, LB, LH and IL with the CH, RH, and RB in covering positions and also available to take part in the passing movement if required. Here opposing players may be drawn towards play. There is plenty of space behind the defenders should any of the attacking mid-field players see an opportunity for a long penetration pass. Further possibilities would arise if one or two players delivered long passes accurately. It may be, for example, that in *fig*. 29 the LH and the IR are the main users for the long pass. Tactically, therefore the forwards who are in an advanced position can expect long through-passes whenever the ball is played to one of these two players. The possibility for pre-arranged tactical moves is greatly increased.

Against a diagonal defense for example we may use the following tactic based upon the LH's ability to deliver a long accurate through-pass (*fig*. 30).

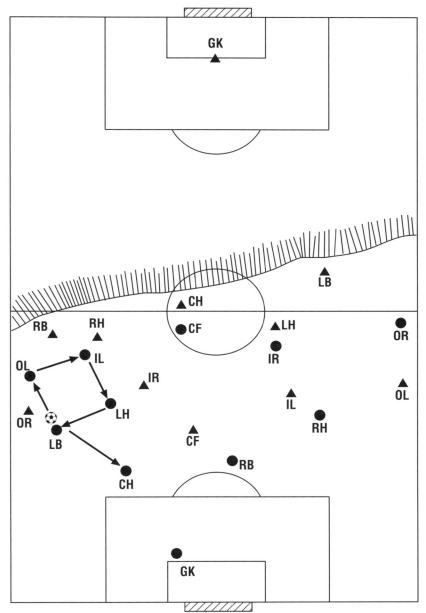

Figure 29

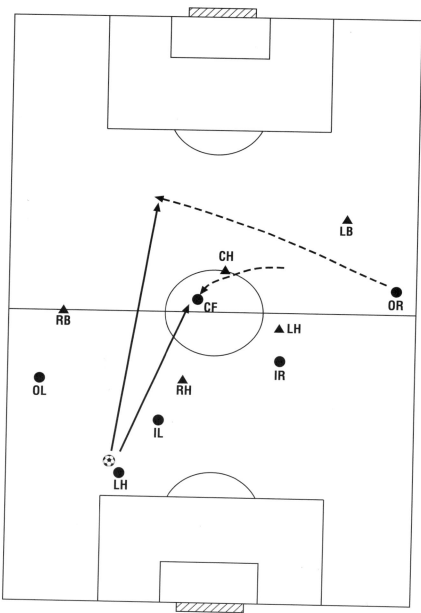

Figure 30

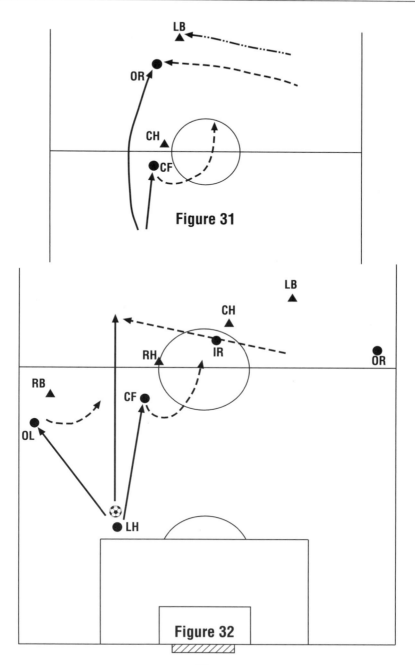

Figure 31

Figure 32

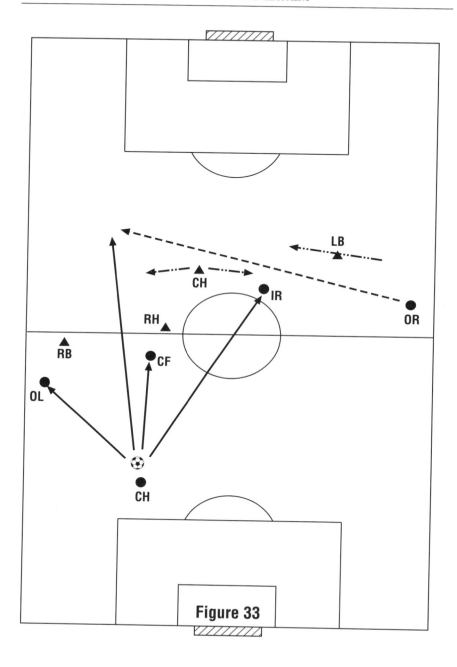

Figure 33

In any defensive structure it is important that the attacking side should, as far as possible, prevent the rear most covering defender from doing his job, which is to cover other defenders. If the OR remains in a deep, wing position the LB can do his job. If, however, by pre-arrangement, the attacking side bases its quick, attacking play on a long pass from the LH, the OR may use a crossfield run in the following way. For any penetration pass there should, if possible, be two alternatives at least. In this situation we may decide that the basic pass shall be a long one from the LH to the feet of the CF who moves into an inside-forward position to receive it. If the OR can time his crossfield run behind the opposing center-half, then our LH has two possibilities—he can use the basic pass to the CF, or he can lengthen his pass over the CF and the opposing center-half's head to his OR (*fig.* 31).

In this way we may have freed the OR in an advanced attacking position. If the LB moves across and marks the OR tightly we have succeeded in playing up to a defender behind whom there is no cover and if the CF is quick to turn inside we have created the possibility of a break-through.

In the same way we might use a long passing build up to the OL (*fig.* 32). Here, against a double center-half system, we have sent one of our forwards onto the covering defender, in this case the CH. This will prevent him from doing his covering job as freely as he would like. This is illustrated in *fig.* 33. Here the IR is only concerned with staying on-side and since the ball and an opponent are in view, this is no problem. The center-half can only move across into a full covering position behind his RB and RH if he is sure that the IR cannot be reached with a pass. To offset this the LB would, of course, swing over to cover the IR. In this case, one could then expect the OR to move across field in search of the through pass.

These long-passing tactics are only really possible when the deliverer of the final pass has time to be accurate and when the potential receivers of his pass have time to see what is likely to happen. Defenders are at a disadvantage because, while they too can see what is likely to happen, they do not know what their opponents are trying to achieve.

We have already seen how retreat and consolidation are basic principles of defensive play. We also know that defensive soccer is relatively easy to organize since it is negative. There is nothing basically creative or imaginative about defense. When teams lack creative players, therefore, they will tend to fall back on heavy defensive organization established quickly in the small area in front of goal. Here, an attacking team will find itself unable to break-through the opposing defense in mid-field; moreover it will be faced by a large numerical superiority near to goal, making certain tactics necessary.

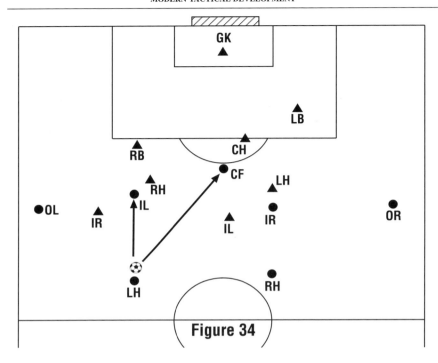

Figure 34

PLAYING ACCURATELY TO FEET

In the less congested area in mid-field, passes can be delivered in front of a player for him to collect in his stride and often at speed. The same sort of pass is necessary in any forceful attacking movement but the nearer the attacking side are to a massed defense, the less will be the scope for making such a pass. Here it becomes vitally important that the build-up of attacking play is by controlled passes made to the feet of forwards. Often the receivers of such passes will be in positions with their backs towards their opponents' goal.

In *fig.* 34 one can see the necessity for accuracy and control in the LH's use of the ball. The passes to the IL and the CF must be made to their feet and with just enough pace to ensure that they are not intercepted. Passes delivered with too much pace will be difficult to control by a player who is tightly marked. At the same time, the ability to play to the feet of tightly marked players is important here. Defenders must mark tightly by moving close to the opposing forward; if they do not, they may give him time to control the ball and shoot for goal. If the player to whom the ball is played

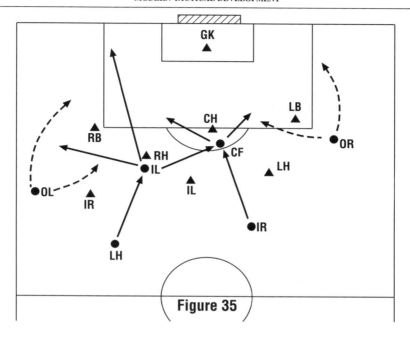

Figure 35

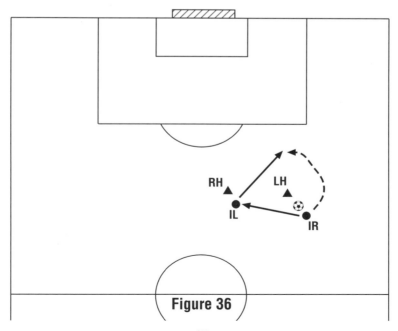

Figure 36

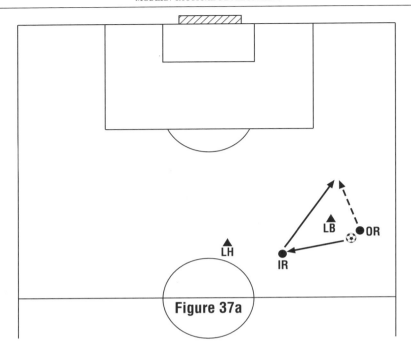

Figure 37a

can control it while using his body as a shield, then there is the possibility for a pass to be pushed or flicked away to on coming attackers. In this way we are using the forward players as rebound surfaces.

SCREENING

This is a technique which is used whereby the body is used to screen the ball from an opponent when the ball is actually in a player's possession or when it comes within playing distance. Against tight marking opponents it is a very necessary skill since it enables a player to hold the ball or to hide his intentions so far as passing the ball is concerned.

We can see how the attacker moves in front of the defender so that his body is always between the defender and the line of the pass. If he is skilled at deflecting the approach pass to other forwards, shooting opportunities can be created (*fig.* 35).

THE WALL PASS

The pass which is deflected by a player who is screening the ball has been likened to the pass a player is returned after kicking a ball against a wall.

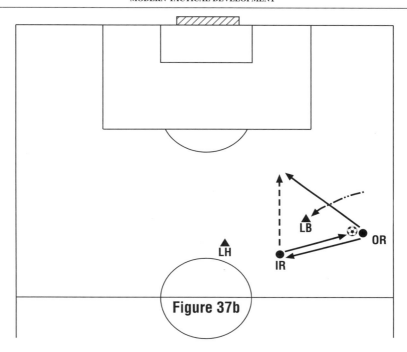

Figure 37b

The angle at which the ball rebounds will vary according to the angle of the pass. The wall pass is often used to exploit a situation where, momentarily, two players are facing one opponent. Alternatively, as in *fig*. 36, where one player is able to pass the ball to a tightly-marked colleague screening the ball from their opponent and returns it at an angle between the two defenders. Many different uses of the wall pass can be practiced to suit various situations.

In *fig*. 37a the orthodox wall pass is given from the IR to the OR who runs behind the LB. In *fig*. 37b LB has moved to cut off this pass and the IR has given a return pass to the OR who now acts as the wall. He pushes the ball at an angle behind the full-back for the IR to run through. The essential factors in a successful wall passing movement are that the player who acts as the wall should be in a position where his partner can make the first pass to him. Secondly, the 'wall' player should be either standing still or moving sideways towards his partner and thirdly, that the return or wall pass should be given first time. The wall pass is executed quickly but it is most effectively employed when the approach play has been slowed down. The change of pace in interpassing movements is a most important technique.

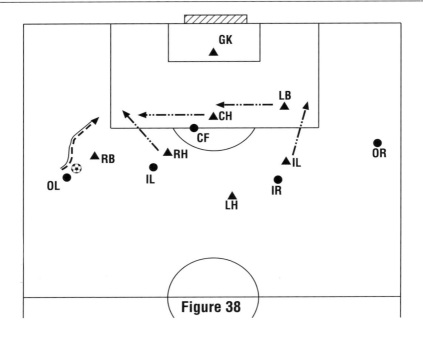

Figure 38

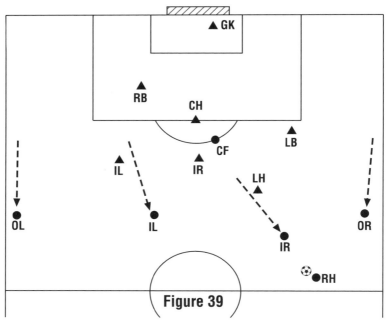

Figure 39

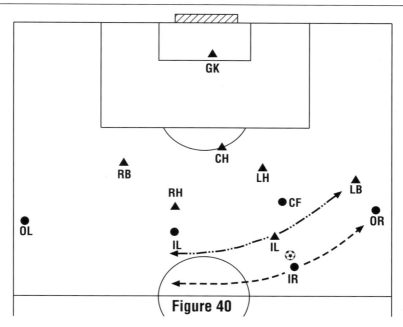

Figure 40

DRIBBLING AND COMMITTING DEFENDERS

Soccer today is an organized and planned game at the very highest levels. While systems of play and tactics are always changing, the extent to which organization can be the basis of success, depends on the skill, understanding, and techniques which are brought to the game by individual players. Thus the technique of beating an opponent by dribbling past him is of ever increasing importance. Players who are capable of taking on opposing players and beating them are capable of causing confusion and chaos in the best organized defenses.

If in the situation (*fig.* 38) the OL can beat the RB, he will cause other defensive players to leave their normal marking positions to try to cover the break-through. This will cause other forwards to be left free. In the past a great deal of emphasis has been placed on attacking players finding open spaces away from defenders. In the modern game these spaces are increasingly difficult to find since defenses are more intensely organized. A defending team will often allow the opposing attackers to find space away from the goal but the nearer to goal attackers move the more space is denied to them.

In *fig.* 39 where the forwards move towards the RH, who has the ball, they may be allowed a fair amount of space. Where they move towards the goal they will find space denied by the concentration of defensive players. In

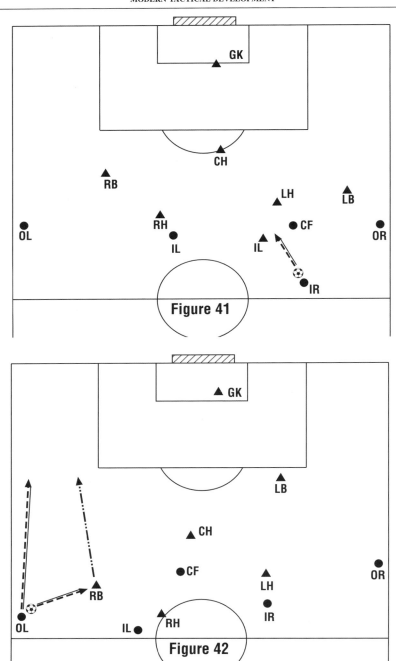

Figure 41

Figure 42

these circumstances, attackers must be prepared to move close to defenders and also to move towards them with the ball, often quickly. We have already seen how screening is an important technique against tightly marking defenders since it can be used to force defenders to make a challenge. In the same way a forward with the ball who is prepared to go straight towards a defender commits him.

In *fig.* 40 the IR in possession moves across the field keeping away from defenders. The opposing IL will shadow him across the field and the rest of the defense behind him will balance accordingly. The IR is not committing the defense or even his immediate opponent in any way.

In *fig.* 41 the IR is moving directly towards the opposing defender (IL) and thus his move will make the IL react in a positive way. Should he fall back or should he make a challenge? The decision is being forced upon him. In the previous situation the IL could afford to wait and see what the developments were likely to be.

In *fig.* 42 where the OL has the ball under control he can move down the line towards the corner-flag. The RB can shadow him and nearby defenders have time to cover and balance accordingly. If the OL, however, suddenly runs at the RB he is forcing the decision onto the full-back. Other defenders must be prepared for a pass or for the OL beating the RB on either side. They are therefore committed to taking positive action.

TACTICS IN DEFENSE

Organization in defense is easy to achieve provided that players fully understand the principles of the game, and this is true at any level of soccer. But it is often disturbing to see schoolboy players moving or standing in certain parts of the field, not because play demands it, but because a misguided although no doubt enthusiastic, teacher or coach has told them to. If young players are not capable of understanding their function in a team, tactics and systems must not be imposed upon them. Imitation without understanding is bad.

Defensive play depends basically on players covering each other and, as we have seen, restricting the amount of time and space which is available to opposing attacking players to work in. Using the three areas of the field which can be identified as:

    1. Attacking area.
    2. Mid-field or build-up area.
    3. Defending area.

we can see how different defensive tactics can be applied.

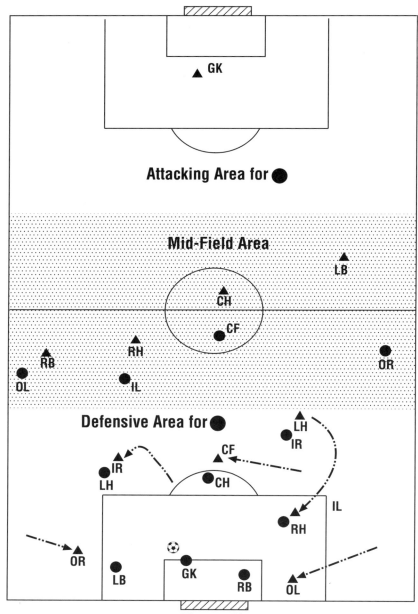

Figure 43

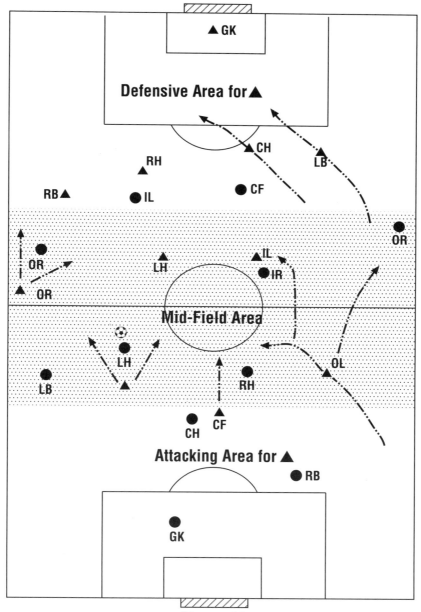

Figure 44

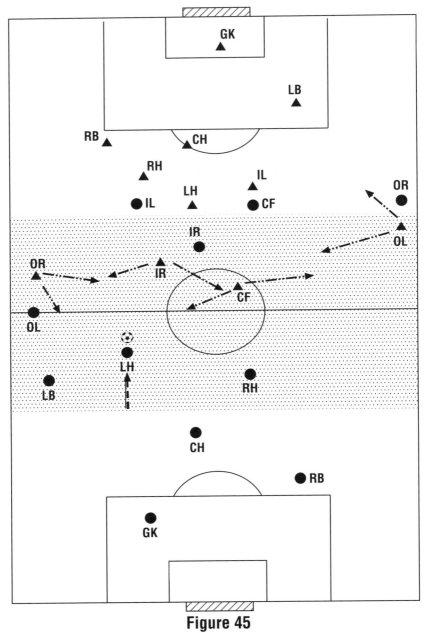

Figure 45

In *fig.* 43 a the attack has broken down in the opponents' penalty-area and the defending goalkeeper has the ball. Obviously, the attacking team's tactics must be to regain possession, if possible, in that attacking area. At the very least they must try to make accurate and controlled use of the ball very difficult for the defending team. The forwards will mark the nearest opposing defenders tightly. Defending players in mid-field will be covered but not so tightly since the further they are away from goal the greater the time available for the offensive players to move and to challenge. If the defending team is now successful in establishing control of the situation, the opposing forwards will continue to pressure them when the ball is near but, at the same time, these forwards will be increasingly conscious of threatening through-passes in the center of the field. They will not all mark quite so tightly. Mid-field players will think principally of retreating in order to make through-passes difficult.

As the opposing attack moves towards the defending area all the attacking players who are immediately concerned with defense will fall back to their defensive zones and more advanced players will begin to look for positions in which they may receive the ball when it has been cleared. Reduced to its simplest forms, defense involves:

    1. Reducing space.

    2. Marking opposing players on a 'man-to-man' basis.

The defensive tactics which we have just studied involve fairly tight man-for-man marking near to the opponents' goal and is known as a half field press. Our aim is to regain possession in our opponents' half of the field and to make it difficult for opposing players to keep possession.

HALF RETREATING DEFENSE

In *fig.* 44 the forwards pressure opponents who are near to them and particularly from behind. The main defensive players retreat slowly so as to make a challenge, if the opportunity occurs, but also to reduce the possibility of effective through-passes being made.

THE FULL RETREATING DEFENSE

In this method of play ball possession determines defensive policy. As soon as the opposition gain possession of the ball (*fig.* 45) the whole team falls back in front of them to produce a series of defensive barriers. The forward barrier threatens the line of through-passes.

More Great Soccer Books from REEDSWAIN

Principles of Team Play

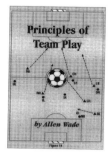

Allen Wade
$8.95

Systems of Play

Allen Wade
$8.95

Dynamic ShortSided Games

Andrew Caruso
$16.95

The Manual of Soccer Coaching

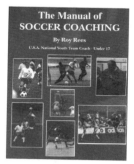

Roy Rees
$14.95

REEDSWAIN INC
To Order Call Toll Free
1-800-331-5191